W9-BLV-408

Dropping In On...

New York City

Hilarie Staton

Rourke
Educational Media

rourkeeducationalmedia.com

Scan for Related Titles
and Teacher Resources

Before Reading:

Building Academic Vocabulary and Background Knowledge

Before reading a book, it is important to tap into what your child or students already know about the topic. This will help them develop their vocabulary, increase their reading comprehension, and make connections across the curriculum.

1. *Look at the cover of the book. What will this book be about?*
2. *What do you already know about the topic?*
3. *Let's study the Table of Contents. What will you learn about in the book's chapters?*
4. *What would you like to learn about this topic? Do you think you might learn about it from this book? Why or why not?*
5. *Use a reading journal to write about your knowledge of this topic. Record what you already know about the topic and what you hope to learn about the topic.*
6. *Read the book.*
7. *In your reading journal, record what you learned about the topic and your response to the book.*
8. *After reading the book complete the activities below.*

Content Area Vocabulary
Read the list. What do these words mean?

borough
harbor
immigrants
island
neighborhoods
population
port
tenement
trade

After Reading:

Comprehension and Extension Activity

After reading the book, work on the following questions with your child or students in order to check their level of reading comprehension and content mastery.

1. *What is New York City best known for? (Summarize)*
2. *What makes New York City such a popular place to visit? (Infer)*
3. *What happened to the Native Americans that lived in the area? (Asking questions)*
4. *What did you learn from this book that you'd never heard anything about? (Text to self connection)*
5. *What do you think it was like in the city on September 11, 2001? (Asking questions)*

Extension Activity

Create a travel brochure about New York City. Include several places visitors should see. Write short, exciting paragraphs that highlight the most interesting things about the city. And don't forget to add pictures! You can draw them or print them out from the Internet.

Table of Contents

United States

VT
MD
NY
CT
New York
PA
NJ

New York City Facts

Founded: New York City (as New Amsterdam): 1626; Renamed New York: 1664; New York City (with five boroughs): 1898

Land area: 304 square miles (787.4 square kilometers)
Elevation: 410 feet (130 meters) above sea level
Previous name: New Amsterdam

Population: 8.5 million
Average Daytime Temperatures:
winter: 41 degrees Fahrenheit (5 degrees Celsius)
spring: 60.5 degrees Fahrenheit (16 degrees Celsius)
summer: 82 degrees Fahrenheit (28 degrees Celsius)
fall: 64 degrees Fahrenheit (18 degrees Celsius)

Ethnic diversity:
African-American 25.5%
American Indian or Alaska Native .7%
Asian 12.7%
Native Hawaiian or Pacific Islander .01%
Hispanic or Latino 28.6%
White 33.3%

City Nicknames:
The City
The Big Apple
Gotham
The City That Never Sleeps
The Melting Pot
The Center of the Universe
The Empire City

New York

New York

Number of Visitors Annually: 56.4 million

Islands and the City

More people live in New York City than any other city in the United States. Its **population** is about 8.5 million.

Most of the city is on islands in the **harbor** where the Atlantic Ocean meets the Hudson River.

These islands used to be covered in forest. Today, a patch of that forest is at the New York Botanical Garden in the Bronx. Some of its trees are 200 years old.

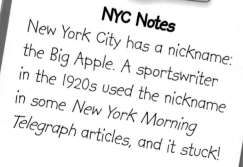

NYC Notes
New York City has a nickname: the Big Apple. A sportswriter in the 1920s used the nickname in some New York Morning Telegraph articles, and it stuck!

New York City is on about 50 islands, including Staten Island, Manhattan Island, and part of Long Island.

American Indians, called the Lenape, fished and hunted on the islands. They greeted Giovanni da Verrazzano (1485–1528), an Italian explorer, when he sailed into the harbor. Later, Henry Hudson (1565–1611), came. He was English, but sailed for the Dutch. He sailed his ship, *The Half Moon*, up the Hudson River.

Many ships still come and go from this harbor.

Henry Hudson was searching for a route to China. He didn't find one. Instead the Dutch began trading with the American Indians.

New York City used to be a small trading town on the tip of Manhattan **Island**. In 1898, 56 cities and towns voted to join together to make one large city. They became the five boroughs, or parts, of New York City.

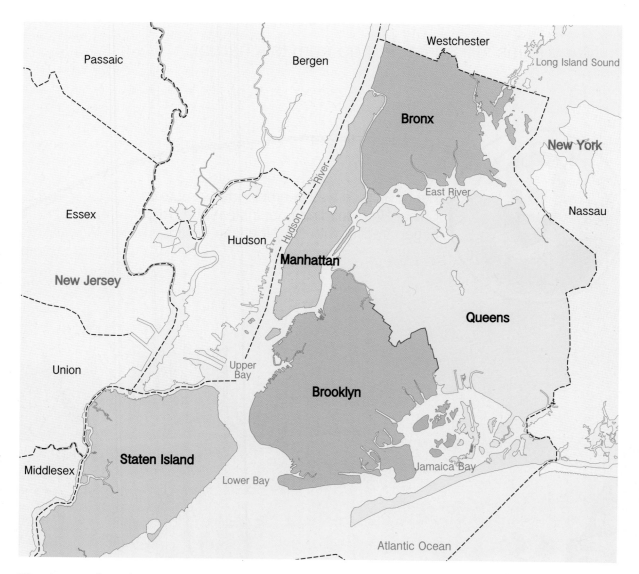

The boroughs of New York City are Manhattan on Manhattan Island, Brooklyn on Long Island, Queens on Long Island, The Bronx on the mainland, and Staten Island.

Manhattan is the smallest **borough**. It has the tallest buildings and the most hotels and offices. Every day, almost four million people pour onto the island. They work in Manhattan, but live somewhere else. Manhattan is the business and government center of New York City.

In the 1920s, many African-American writers and musicians moved to Harlem, a neighborhood in Manhattan. Many African-American stars began by performing at Harlem's Apollo Theater.

At first, farms in The Bronx sold food to people in Manhattan. Its population grew quickly after a subway was built.

The Bronx is on the mainland of New York state. Over half its people speak a language at home that is not English. On its streets, you hear both Latin and hip hop music.

BROOKLYN NEIGHBORHOODS ARE CHANGING BECAUSE MANY YOUNG, CREATIVE PEOPLE NOW LIVE IN THEM.

Brooklyn has more people than any other borough, and many of its residents work in Manhattan.

Queens is the biggest borough. Over two million people live there. Many are **immigrants**, people from one country who move to live in another. People speak about 160 different languages in Queens.

Staten Island has the smallest population. Until 1964, you had to take a ferry from Staten Island to any other part of the city. In 1964, the Verrazano-Narrows Bridge was built between Brooklyn and Staten Island.

Riders on the Staten Island Ferry have great views of the Manhattan skyline, the Statue of Liberty, and Ellis Island.

People live in the tall buildings around Central Park. The park is their backyard.

New York City has 1,700 parks. Central Park is in Manhattan. The builders created a huge park on swamps and pig farms. It has trails, lakes, and playgrounds. It has a zoo and a carousel with handmade horses.

Rhinoceroses, tortoises, and Komodo dragons live at the
Bronx Zoo's Zoo Center, which was built to look like a palace.

Every borough has a zoo. The biggest is the Bronx Zoo. Most of
its animals are not in cages. People stand behind glass to watch
gorillas and tigers.

At the American Museum of Natural History in Manhattan, you
can take a trip into space, walk among live butterflies, and see
how people lived long ago.

A statue in front of the Museum of Natural History
honors President Theodore Roosevelt because he
worked to protect the environment and wildlife.

NYC Notes
The Bronx Zoo opened to the public in 1899. It is the largest metropolitan zoo in the United States.

11

Moving People and Goods

From its beginning, New York City was a place of business. The Lenape Indians traded their goods with other American Indians who lived nearby. When the Dutch wanted the land, they paid using **trade** goods such as beads, knives, and cloth. American Indians brought animal skins to Dutch traders. Farmers brought grain to the city. After the grain was turned into flour, it was sent to other towns.

Immigrants came to the city from many places. When the British took over the city at the start of the American Revolution, it grew even faster.

NYC Notes
New York City was the capital of the United States when George Washington became the country's first president in 1789.

The British Army controlled New York City and its harbor during the American Revolution, which lasted from 1765-1783. Battles were fought in Brooklyn and Manhattan Island.

Ships sailed into the beautiful harbor. They brought people and goods. They took away animal skins, flour, and wood.

Old streets of stones still run along the harbor at the South Street Seaport. There you can explore the decks and cabins of six historic ships. The area is now a designated historic district with some of the oldest buildings in downtown Manhattan.

THE SOUTH STREET SEAPORT MUSEUM HAS THE LARGEST PRIVATELY OWNED FLEET OF HISTORIC SHIPS IN THE UNITED STATES.

The *Peking*, built in 1911, is one of six historic ships docked at the South Street Seaport.

The first trains came into the city in the 1830s. Horses pulled them. Then came steam trains, which were dirty and dangerous.

Grand Central Depot was built far from where people lived. The city grew around the station. It's now called Grand Central Terminal. It has many tunnels and 67 tracks deep underground. The ceiling in the main concourse has 2,500 lights that look like stars in the sky. About 750,000 people use it every day.

Grand Central Terminal is the third station built on the site. It opened in 1913. The original station, called Grand Central Depot, opened in 1871.

For years, people had to take a boat or ferry to get from one borough to another. Not anymore! Cars, trucks, and trains rumble across bridges and tunnels. You can even walk across some of the bridges.

The Brooklyn Bridge, which connects Brooklyn and Manhattan, was the world's first steel suspension bridge when it opened in 1883.

The Lincoln Tunnel also runs under the Hudson River, connecting New York and New Jersey. It opened in 1937.

The Holland Tunnel stretches under the Hudson River, connecting New York and New Jersey. It opened in 1927.

Subways are the quickest way to get around New York City. The subways become really crowded when people are traveling to and from work each day.

In 1900, the city began to dig tunnels for a subway, or underground train. It makes stops under the city streets. The subway grew. It is now about 660 miles (1,062 kilometers). If you put all its tracks end-to-end they would reach from New York City to Chicago, Illinois!

Soaring Skyscrapers

Both old and new skyscrapers reach to the sky in Manhattan. When you stand on the sidewalk, it feels as if you are in a canyon of buildings. New York City has more skyscrapers in one place than anywhere else in the world.

Built in 1930, the Chrysler Building is still one of the world's most beautiful buildings, both inside and out.

The Empire State building opened in 1931. For 40 years it was the tallest building in the world. It has 73 elevators to race up 102 floors. From there you can look across the city. The tower is illuminated by lights.

The Empire State building has so many offices, it has its own zip code.

Most countries of the world belong to The United Nations. It tries to keep peace and help people worldwide. The organization is based in New York City. People from almost every country in the world work there.

On September 11, 2001, airplanes were flown into the World Trade Center towers. Both buildings fell. Although many people escaped, nearly 3,000 died. Near the new World Trade building, called One World Trade Center, is a memorial, or a place to remember. It lists all those who died that day.

In 1973, the World Trade Center was finished. Each of its twin towers had 110 stories. For two years they were the world's tallest buildings.

The Statue of Liberty was a gift from the people of France. It arrived in 350 pieces that had to be put together.

In 1886, the Statue of Liberty opened. She sits on an island in New York Harbor. Miss Liberty stands for the freedom to begin a new life. She greets every ship that arrives. She was repaired for her 100th birthday. Now you can climb all the way to her crown and look out over New York Harbor.

Near Lady Liberty is Ellis Island. Immigrants went to Ellis Island before they were allowed on the mainland. Today, the Ellis Island Immigration Museum tells the story of those who passed through its doors.

New York City has many cultural festivals, including the Puerto Rican Day Parade.

Over the years, many immigrants made New York City their home. Today, it is filled with immigrant **neighborhoods**. Russians live in Brighton Beach, Brooklyn. Puerto Ricans live in the South Bronx. There is a Chinatown in Manhattan, Queens, and another in Brooklyn.

In these places, immigrants live near other people from their native countries. You hear them speaking their home languages. Restaurants serve food from that country. It might be Indian curry or Turkish lamb.

Companies built factories in New York City. They knew there were lots of workers there. For many years, New York City had more factories and more workers than any other city in the country.

In the early 1900s, many immigrant workers made clothes. They sewed clothes at home or in a factory. They were paid a little bit for each piece they made. Because they were paid so little, the whole family had to work.

NYC Notes
In New York City a new type of building, called a **tenement**, housed many immigrants. Whole families lived in small, cramped spaces. Sometimes they all worked and slept in the same room.

The Lower East Side Tenement Museum, a National Historic site, tells the stories of New York City's immigrants.

What to Do?

In 1930, John D. Rockefeller, Jr. (1874–1960) created a "city within a city." Rockefeller Center has 19 buildings. Some are on the famous shopping street, Fifth Avenue. In one building they film NBC television shows. Radio City Music Hall is in another. That's where The Rockettes have been kicking up their legs since 1925.

Ice skating at the world-famous rink at Rockefeller Center has been a New York City tradition since 1936.

Not far from Rockefeller Center is Times Square. Bright signs flash news. Huge pictures of movie and TV stars stare down at you. Lights are everywhere.

Times Square has stores that are so big, one has a Ferris wheel inside it.

Broadway is famous for its theaters. There are shows for everyone. The actors, singers, and dancers make the shows come alive.

In New York City, plays might have singing or dancing. Another theater will have music, ballet, or even Chinese acrobats.

Central Park has exhibits each year featuring its many sculptures and other genres of art that are open to the public.

Art is all over New York City. Find the statue of Alice in Wonderland in Central Park. A giant rose and paintings of soup cans are at the Museum of Modern Art. El Museo del Barrio has lots to see. Many of its artists are from Puerto Rico.

There are many other art museums, like the Metropolitan Museum of Art and the Brooklyn Museum. They have famous paintings and statues from all over the world.

People in New York City like sports, but they love their baseball teams! They've had four major league teams over the years.

Jackie Robinson
(1919–1972)

Many people loved the Brooklyn Dodgers. They were the first major league team to have an African-American player, Jackie Robinson. But in 1957, their owner moved the team to Los Angeles. Many people never forgave them. At the same time, another New York team, the Giants, moved to San Francisco.

The New York Yankees still play in the Bronx. They have been world champs 27 times. The Mets came to Queens in 1964.

Millions of New Yorkers go to baseball games every year to cheer for their favorite team.

New York has special celebrations that no other city has.

Millions come to see the Macy's Thanksgiving Day Parade. Huge character-shaped balloons glide high above the street. The first balloon was Felix the Cat in 1927.

On the Fourth of July, Coney Island hosts the Nathan's Hot Dog Eating Contest. Later, a huge fireworks display fills the sky over the harbor. Many people watch from boats or from one of the many bridges.

On New Year's Eve, Times Square is filled with thousands of people. At midnight a giant ball slowly drops. Everyone counts down. When it reaches the bottom the lights flash. People cheer to welcome in the New Year.

Timeline

1524
Lenape Indians greet Italian explorer Giovanni da Verrazzano.

1609
Henry Hudson sails into New York Harbor.

1776-1783
The British Army controls New York City.

1832
First trains on Manhattan Island.

1871
Cornelius Vanderbilt builds the first Grand Central Station.

1898
Towns and cities join together to create a much bigger New York City.

1931
Empire State Building opens.

1973
World Trade Center Towers finished.

2001
World Trade Center Towers destroyed.

2011
Superstorm Sandy hits New York City.

Glossary

borough (BUR-oh): an area of a city that has its own government

harbor (HAHR-bur): an area of calm water near land where ships can safely dock and unload cargo

immigrants (IM-i-gruhnts): people who move from one country to settle in another

island (EYE-luhnd): land completely surrounded by water

neighborhoods (NAY-bur-huds): sections of a city where people live

population (pahp-yuh-LAY-shuhn): the number of people who live in a place

port (port): a place where ships can dock to load and unload goods and materials

tenement (TEN-uh-muhnt): a crowded building divided into small apartments and often in the poor part of a city

trade (trade): buying and selling goods or exchanging one thing for another

Index

Show What You Know

1. Which of New York City's five boroughs are on islands?

2. How do people travel between New York City's boroughs?

3. How have New York's buildings changed?

4. What is special about the city's immigrant neighborhoods?

5. Name five places you'd like to visit in New York City.

Websites to Visit

collections.mcny.org/Explore/Themes

www.centralparknyc.org/things-to-see-and-do

www.nyhistory.org/childrens-museum/clubhouse

About the Author

Hilarie Staton used to live in Brooklyn. She still lives near the city. She goes into New York City every chance she gets. She loves its museums, shows, festivals, and stores. She has written books about the Statue of Liberty, Ellis Island, and New York State history.

Meet The Author!
www.meetREMauthors.com

www.rourkeeducationalmedia.com

PHOTO CREDITS: Cover: © Songquan Deng, OlegAlbinsky, Veni, JJRD; Page 4: © pidjoe; Page 5: © Eliza Snow; Page 7: © Rolf_52; Page 8: © Lee Snider, Terraxplorer; Page 9: © MSHCH; Page 10: © Songquan Deng, wdstock; Page 11: © Littleny, Sean Pavone; Page 13: © eyfoto; Page 14: © Jorg Hackemann; Page 15: © blindfoldstudios, Anna Bryukhanova, Christina Muraca; Page 16: © Marek Slusarczyk; Page 17: © Matjaz Boncina; Page 18: © BluemoonPics, uca headquarters: Page 19: © robert paul van beets; Page 20: © Chris Parypa; Page 21: © lev radin; Page 22: © wdstock; Page 23: © titoslack; Page 24: © duha127; Page 25: © infusny-236/Corbis; Page 26: © wdstock; Page 27: © U.S. National Archives and Records Administration, gary yim; Page 28: © Anna Bryukhanova; Page 29: © Library of Congress, Sergey Borisov, Marc, Marcus Linstrom, van beets, Jay Lazarin

Edited by: Keli Sipperley

Illustrations by: Caroline Romanet

Cover and interior design by: Jen Thomas

Library of Congress PCN Data

Dropping in on New York City/ Hilarie Staton
ISBN 978-1-68191-403-9 (hard cover)
ISBN 978-1-68191-445-9 (soft cover)
ISBN 978-1-68191-483-1 (e-Book)
Library of Congress Control Number: 2015951569

Also Available as:

Printed in the United States of America, North Mankato, Minnesota